Beautiful
BEAD
WEAVING

Simple Techniques and Patterns for
Creating Stunning Loom Jewelry

Fran Ortmeyer & Carol C. Porter

DESIGN ORIGINALS
an Imprint of Fox Chapel Publishing
www.d-originals.com

© 2015 by Fran Ortmeyer, Carol C. Porter, and New Design Originals Corporation, www.d-originals.com, an imprint of Fox Chapel Publishing, 800-457-9112, 903 Square Street, Mount Joy, PA 17552.

Beautiful Bead Weaving is a collection of new and previously published material. Portions of this book have been reproduced from *Bead Weaving on a Loom* (978-1-57421-384-3).

We are always looking for talented authors. To submit an idea, please send a brief inquiry to acquisitions@foxchapelpublishing.com.

Printed in China

Second printing

Acknowledgments

To our publisher and editors, thank you for your patience and encouragement through the process. Not just one person puts together a book, and we would like to thank all those behind the scenes.

I would like to give a special thank you to Carol Porter, who gave direction and guidance throughout this process and graciously shared her knowledge and insight with me.

To my husband, for changing his schedules to allow me time for this exciting project, and family members who were constantly supportive and encouraging.

To those of you that will use this book to create your own beautiful projects—I wish I could see each and every creation!

—

Thank you Jan Carr for nudging us in this direction, and Judith McCabe and Peg Couch for "cheerleading" this project.

Always thanks to my David for your unending support during the time of this writing.

A special thanks to TOHO Beads for contributing your beautiful beads, some illustrations, and great support.

—

Introduction

Everyone has within them the seed of creativity. It finds a way to blossom in whatever medium you choose to work. Beading with the Clover Loom has opened a new world within which I can express emotions and colors that define what creativity is for me.

With the introduction of Clover's Mini Loom the creative possibilities are endless. The challenge of putting these smaller units together to create unique finished pieces of jewelry is exciting and fun.

—Fran

My first recollection of beaded loom work was feeling the silkiness of my mother's evening bag and the smooth band of beads in a childhood bracelet made by a Native American artisan. Working on Clover's standard bead weaving loom is an adventure of "what if" possibilities. With so many configurations and capacities that this loom can employ my creative nature is having a field day! From a small pair of earrings to an endless amount of warp for a necklace or hat band, I can accomplish so much on just this one loom.

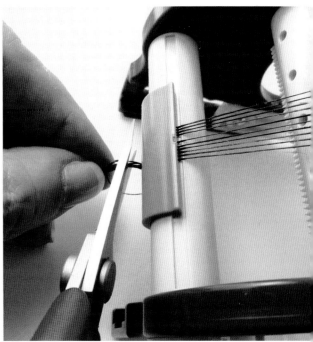

The Mini Loom, or credit card-sized loom as I like to call it, is a grand idea coming from Clover Needlecraft. This loom allows the most novice of bead enthusiasts the opportunity to try his or her hand at loom work. Unintimidating and straightforward small pieces such as earrings, pins, and medallions can be made in minutes. We can think beyond a final and complete piece to segments for use in bracelets and necklaces to small embellishments on cross stitch, needlepoint, and other handmade items—again the only limitation is your own creativity. When I want to try out a design or test warp and bead color combinations, this mini loom is my go-to loom to view possible results before warping the standard loom. Beading on a loom has provided me many hours of fascinating designs and rewarding results.

—Carol

This book is designed to answer as many questions as one might have about loom work, and give many techniques and designs for you to begin to feel comfortable with both looms. We trust this book will be for you the gateway to a world of creative endeavors!

Contents

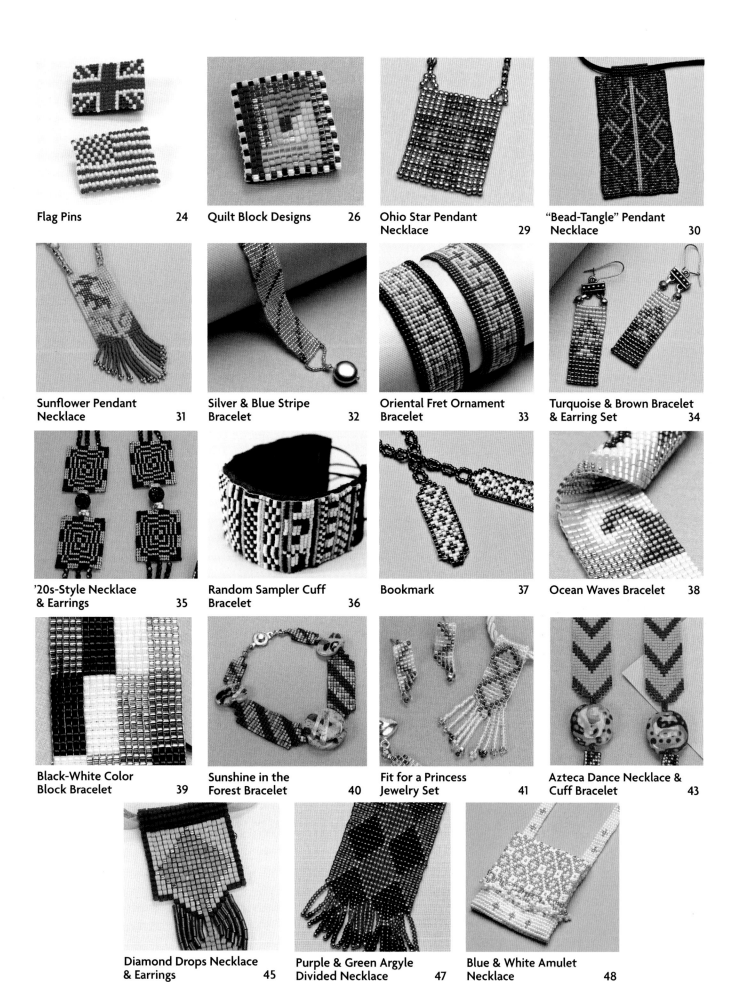

Materials & Supplies

Thread: We recommend 100 percent polyester thread, #60, in neutral colors like white, gray, beige, black, brown, and dark green. This fiber does not stretch or break, both great features for loom work. Nylon monofilament thread, such as Nymo size B, works well and comes in a variety of colors. We have also used Superlon thread, also known as S-lon, with great results.

Neutral colors, such as black, white, tan, and gray can be used for the warp threads. We recommend using weft threads in colors that coordinate with whatever bead color falls to the outside edges of the woven piece, as this will help hide the thread. If desired, a permanent maker can always be used to color the outer threads to match the beads. Be cautious when using transparent beads, as the thread color may distort or enhance the original bead color.

Needles: Generally, a long thin needle with a narrow eye works best for loom work. We use Clover Needlecraft Incorporated's Beading Needles numbers 10–13. In addition, a simple needle threader is handy for ushering the thread through the needle eye, and a short needle is useful for hiding warp threads.

Seed beads: Seed beads are a class of beads that are the smallest glass beads—not all seed beads are created equal! Common sizes include 15/0, 11/0, 8/0, and 6/0. We've found that Japanese seed beads are the most uniform, making them the best for weaving. In addition, the depth of color range and finishes for these beads is most extensive. Uniform beads result in elegant and even loom work with a silky, smooth texture. Using different types of seed beads in one weaving will throw off the uniformity of the finished piece.

The projects in this book use size 11/0 seed beads exclusively. These beads come in two bead shapes, round and cylindrical (a slightly squared cylinder), and each project will indicate which type is used.

Scissors: Choose a small pair of scissors with a nice sharp tip.

The bracelet on the left uses 11/0 round beads, while the bracelet on the right uses 11/0 cylindrical beads. Note the difference in finished size. The cylindrical bead bracelet is smaller, even though both bracelets use 11/0 beads.

The outer edges of the right bracelet are uneven, due to mixing round and cylindrical beads. The left bracelet uses all cylindrical beads, resulting in a uniform, professional look.

Here, light silver round beads have been used in a design that also contains cylindrical beads. As a result of using two different types of beads, the rows are becoming uneven.

The Mini Loom Basics

This loom is small but mighty! It's easy to transport and warp, making it perfect for whipping up projects quickly. The workspace is limited so you can focus on creating earrings, necklace medallions, pins, and small connecting units for necklaces and bracelets. It's a good tool to use for a quick test of designs, bead styles, and colorations.

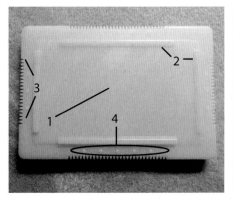
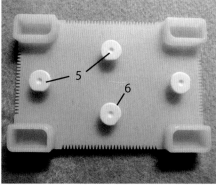
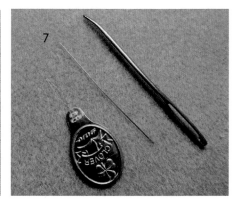

Parts Names and Functions

1. Workspace (weaving area)
2. Bars (lift warp threads off surface)
3. Grooves (separate and hold warp strands to match bead width; loom can support 30 warp strands [29 beads] horizontally, 20 warp strands [19 beads] vertically)
4. Guide indicators (small dots to help guide warp strands to matching grooves on opposite side)
5. Stoppers (4 pieces for securing thread ends)
6. Posts (for wrapping warp thread when warping the loom; shown covered by stoppers, see uncovered on page 9)
7. Additional parts: threader, beading needle, darning needle

Getting Started

Determine the design. Based on the size of the piece, decide whether to use the loom horizontally or vertically. Use it horizontally for wide and short pieces, vertically for thin and long pieces.

Determine the number of warp strands. The number of beads in the widest row of the design, plus 1, equals the number of warp strands needed to warp the loom. For example, a design that is 10 beads wide requires 11 warp strands.

Determine the warping method. Warping the mini loom follows the same method as warping the standard loom using the Continuous Warp Method (see page 9 to learn how to warp the mini loom and page 13 to learn how to warp the standard loom). The posts on the back of the mini loom have the same function as the pegs on the standard loom.

The Continuous Warp Method

Warp the Mini Loom

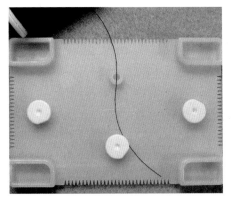

1 On the back of the loom, remove the stopper from the top post and place the thread over the post.

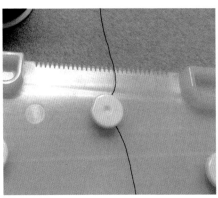

2 Replace the stopper to secure the thread.

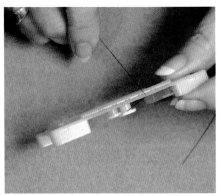

3 Find the starting groove. Bring the thread from the back of the loom to the front and insert the thread in the starting groove at the top of the loom.

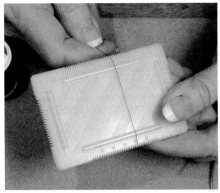

4 Bring the thread down to the bottom edge of the loom and secure it in the groove directly opposite the starting groove.

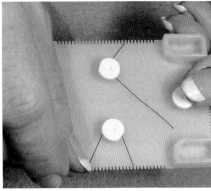

5 Wind the thread around the post on the back of the loom, opposite the starting post.

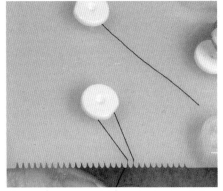

6 Bring the thread from the back of the loom to the front and insert the thread in the next groove.

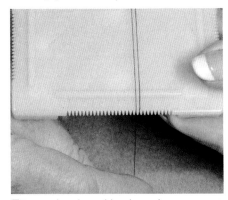

7 Bring the thread back to the top edge of the loom and secure it in the groove directly opposite the one on the bottom edge.

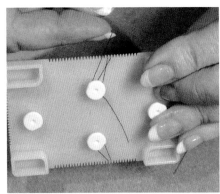

8 Wind the thread around the starting post on the back of the loom. Repeat Steps 3–8 to continue warping the loom until you have created the number of warp strands necessary for your project.

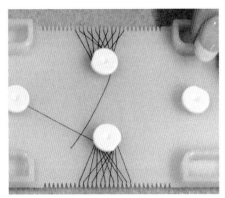

9 Wind the thread around the last post. Then, secure the thread end on an unused post (see Steps 1 & 2) and trim it.

Weaving with the Mini Loom

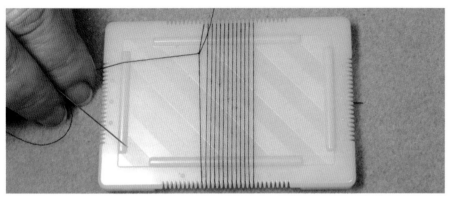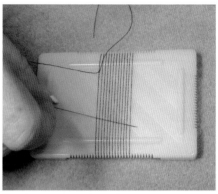

1 Thread the weft thread onto a beading needle, leaving a 4" (10cm) tail. Tie the loose end onto the leftmost warp thread.

2 Lift the warp threads using the darning needle and pass the beading needle UNDER the warp threads (from left to right). Then pick up the beads for the first row.

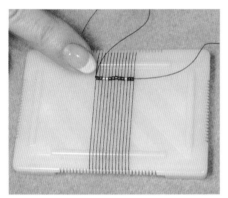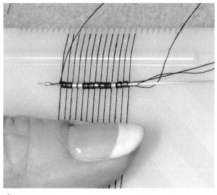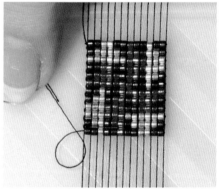

3 Place the beads between the warp threads and remove darning needle.

4 Push down on the warp threads so the beads pop out above them. Now slide the needle back through the beads (from right to left), needle eye first, making sure the needle passes OVER all of the warp threads.

5 Repeat Steps 2–4 to continue adding rows of beads until your design is complete. After you have finished the last row, tie the weft thread to the warp thread.

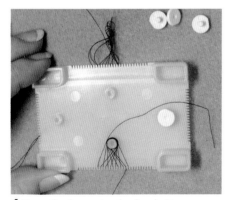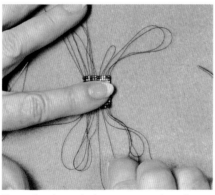

6 Turn the loom to the back. Remove all of the stoppers and slide the warp threads off the posts.

7 For finishing, hiding warp and weft threads, and increasing and decreasing, follow the methods described for the standard loom on pages 15-16 and 20.

The Standard Loom Basics

Part Names and Functions

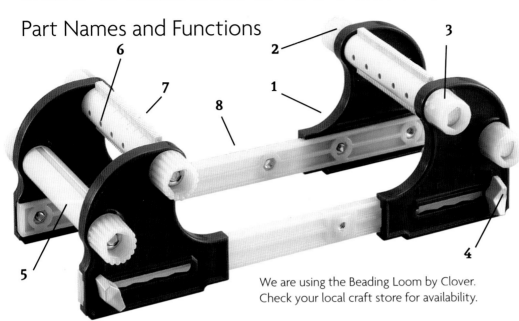

We are using the Beading Loom by Clover. Check your local craft store for availability.

1. Frame
2. Release knobs A (loosen or tighten the beams)
3. Release knobs B (rotate the beams)
4. Adjustment screws (allow adjustment of rail length between warp guide beams)
5. Winding beams (keep ends of warp threads in place and wind long pieces)
6. Peg holes (for use with the Continuous Warp Method, see page 13)
7. Warp guide beams (beams with grooves to guide the warp threads)
8. Rails

Grooves

The warp guide beams contain two different types of grooves:

Grooves (a): Use for cylinder beads (size 11/0). The maximum width of your woven piece will be about 2⁹⁄₁₆" (6.5cm) wide, or 43 beads across (44 warp threads).

Grooves (b): Use for round beads (size 11/0). The maximum width of your woven piece will be about 2½" (6.5cm) wide, or 39 beads across (40 warp threads). Grooves (b) can be identified by the horizontal line running along the base of the grooves.

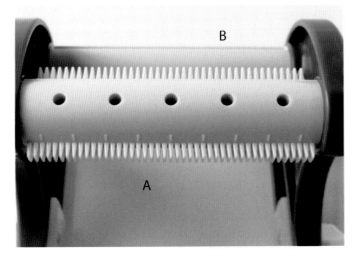

The warp guide beam contains two different types of grooves for working with different types of beads: grooves a (bottom), and grooves b (top).

Additional parts

Pegs (12 pcs.): Use for Continuous Warp Method (see page 13)

Warp thread stoppers (2 pcs.): Insert stopper into holes in the grooves on the warp guide beam. Keeps the warp threads from popping off the grooves while loom is in use or moved.

Non-slip strips (4 pcs.): Stick on bottom of loom to prevent slippage while weaving.

Holders (4 pcs.): Use these to keep warp threads in place on winding beam. Also, use serrated edge to untangle warp threads.

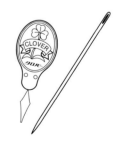

Beading needle No. 10 and threader (1 pc.)

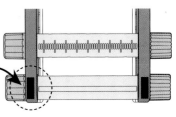

How to Adjust the Loom

Use the indicators on the rails and elongated slits to adjust the length of the loom in ⅜" (1cm) units.

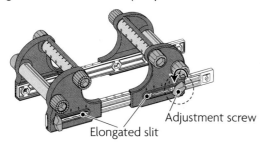

Adjustment screw
Elongated slit

1 Loosen right and left adjustment screws.

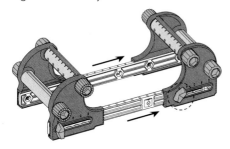

2 Move frames to desired length.

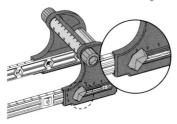

3 Set frames at the desired length; then tighten adjustment screws on both sides. Make sure the frame is set at the same position on both rails before tightening the screws.

Shortest position: 2¼" (5.5cm)

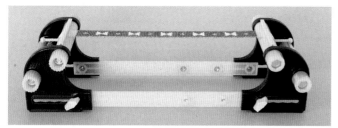

Longest position: 8⅜" (21.5cm)

How to Use Release Knobs A & B

1 Loosen beam with Knob A (counter clockwise).

2 Rotate beam with Knob B.

3 Tighten beam with Knob A, making sure the beam is firmly set.

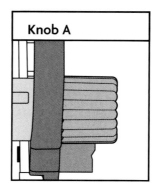

Knob A

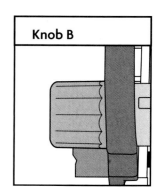

Knob B

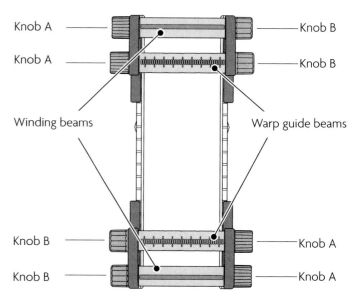

Knob A
Knob A
Knob B
Knob B

Winding beams
Warp guide beams

Knob B
Knob B
Knob A
Knob A

Important!

Check the knobs to make sure they are firmly tightened while weaving. Loose knobs may result in uneven weaving.

The Continuous Warp Method

Warp the Standard Loom

Use this warping method for shorter woven pieces, 7½" (19cm) long or less.

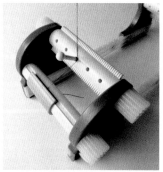

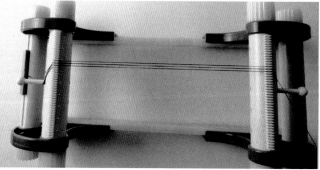

1 Adjust the length of the loom to fit the piece you plan to weave. Insert a peg in one of the peg holes in each warp guide beam.

2 Secure one end of the warp thread on the winding beam with a holder, and loop the thread around the peg 2–3 times to start the warping process.

3 Place the warp thread into a groove on the warp guide beam and extend the thread to the corresponding groove on the opposite beam, looping it around the peg from left to right. Repeat until you have the necessary number of warp strands. Note: The number of warps strands required will be 1 more than the number of beads you plan to use across the body of your work, so a project 11 beads wide requires 12 warp strands.

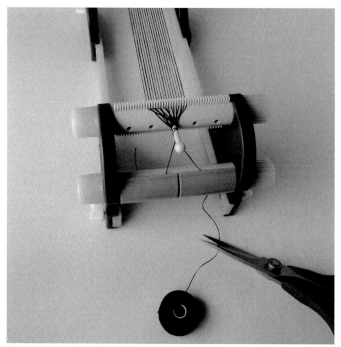

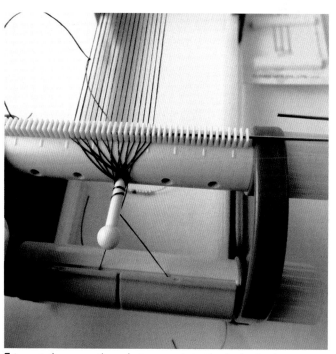

4 After placing the required number of warp strands, loop the end of the warp thread around the closest peg 2–3 times. Secure the thread on the closest winding beam with a holder and trim the end.

5 Insert the warp thread stoppers into the holes in the grooves of each warp guide beam. This will keep the warp threads from popping out of the grooves.

Weaving with the Standard Loom

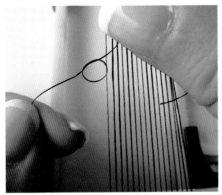

1 Thread the weft thread onto a beading needle, leaving a 4" (10cm) tail. Tie the loose end onto the leftmost warp thread.

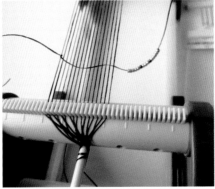

2 Bring the weft thread UNDER the warp threads and pick up the beads for the first row.

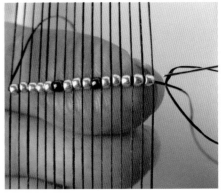

3 Press the beads up against the warp threads, positioning one bead between each warp thread, starting from the left.

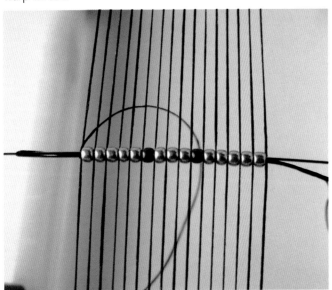

4 While continuing to hold the beads in place against the warp threads, slide the needle back through beads, needle eye first, making sure the needle passes OVER all of the warp threads.

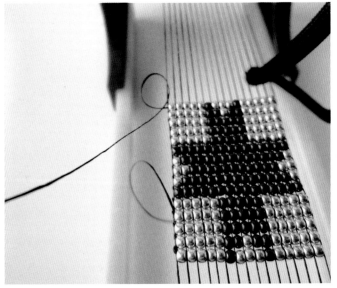

5 Repeat Steps 2–4 to continue adding rows of beads until your design is complete. After you have finished the last row, tie the weft thread to the warp thread.

Important!

When you pass the eye of the needle through the beads, always bring it OVER the warp threads.

Hiding Warp & Weft Threads

Method A

Use this finishing method for a project that uses one continuous thread as the warp and has no increases or decreases.

1 To remove the woven piece from the standard loom, release the warp beams, remove the holders, and then remove the pegs. For the mini loom, remove all of the stoppers and slide the warp threads off the posts.

2 Place the woven piece on a flat surface. Divide the warp threads at the center.

3 Pull strand 1 downward gently, as shown in Figure 1.

4 Pull strand 2 upward (see Figure 1). Repeat Steps 3 and 4 until you reach the left edge of the piece.

5 Repeat the same process on the right side, working out from the center as you did before (see Figure 2).

6 To hide the warp threads that have been pulled through the piece, thread the end of the left thread onto a beading needle. Pass the needle through the second bead from the left side, going through 2 or 3 beads. Pass needle through 4 to 5 rows of the weft threads, picking up the UPPER weft threads. Pass the needle through a row of beads from left to right, going through the second bead from the right side. Then, pass the needle through the next row of beads, going back to the left. Cut thread at the edge of the second to last bead in the row (see Figure 3). Repeat with the remaining warp thread.

7 Hide the weft threads at the beginning and end of the woven piece as shown in Figure 4.

Weaver's Knot

When you run out of weft thread, join more thread by using the Weaver's Knot. Make sure the knot slips inside the beads.

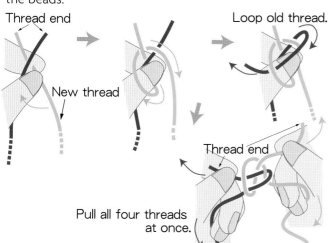

Thread end

New thread

Loop old thread.

Thread end

Pull all four threads at once.

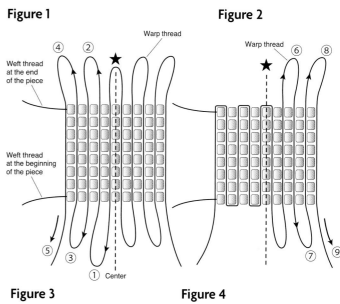

Figure 1

Warp thread

Weft thread at the end of the piece

Weft thread at the beginning of the piece

④ ② ★

⑤ ③

① Center

Figure 2

Warp thread

★ ⑥ ⑧

⑦ ⑨

Figure 3

Figure 4

Upper weft thread

Lower weft thread

Bead

Warp thread

Important!

We cannot express strongly enough here that if the warp threads do not pull easily STOP. Try following Method B on page 16, which requires the warp threads only be pulled downward through the piece. If it is not possible to pull the warp threads through the piece at all, trim the warp thread loops, keeping the threads long enough to be threaded onto a needle. Then, follow the method described on page 19 to hide the individual warp threads in the woven piece.

Method B

Use this finishing method for a project with a continuous warp thread and increases or decreases on only one end of the woven piece. The warp threads will all be pulled downward toward the increase/decrease end, cut, and then woven back into the piece.

1 Remove the woven piece from the loom and place it on a flat surface. Pull threads 1–3 downward toward the end with the increase or decrease, following the arrows in Figure 1. Do NOT pull on the outer warp threads (labeled A and B). Continue pulling strands 1–3 downward gently until the thread loops meet the beads in the top row without causing it to pucker. Cut the thread loops at the bottom (see Figure 2).

2 Thread one of the outer warp threads on a beading needle. If the piece has increases or decreases, pick up UPPER weft threads for several rows, starting at the first full row. Then, run the needle through the closest row of beads, bringing it out at the side. Cut the thread at the edge of the second to last bead in the row. Hide the remaining outer warp thread in the same way (see Figure 3).

3 With the exception of the threads marked with stars, hide the remaining wrap threads using the method described in Step 2 (see Figure 4).

4 The starred threads are on the last row. To hide these threads, thread them on a beading needle. Then, pick up the UPPER weft threads for several rows, starting with the second to last row (see Figure 5). Run the needle through a row of beads as shown in Figure 3, and trim the excess thread.

5 Hide the weft threads at the beginning and end of the woven piece as shown in Figure 4 of Method A on page 15.

Figure 1

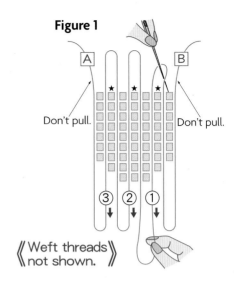

Figure 2

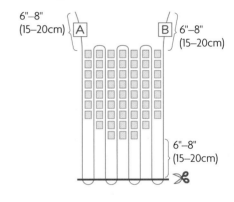

Figure 3

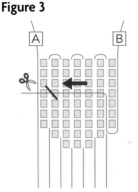

Tip

When moving the needle horizontally, avoid passing it through the same beads twice.

Figure 4

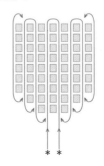

Figure 5

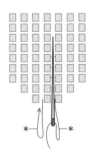

Glossary of Terms

If you're new to beading or bead weaving, you might not be as familiar with some of the terms used in this book. Here is a short list of the most important terms you'll need to know:

Warp: The series of threads that run lengthwise through a woven piece and are held in place by a frame or loom.

Weft: The working thread woven widthwise through the warp of a woven piece; in bead weaving, the thread used to attach beads to the warp.

Round beads: These are seed beads with a rounded shape.

Cylindrical beads: These are seed beads with a slightly square shape.

Increases/Decreases:
A project is said to have increases or decreases when the number of beads per row is raised or lowered, usually at the beginning and end of the project.

Bead tips: These are used to finish the end of a piece by enclosing the working strands. They also provide a way to attach a clasp to a project. See how to attach a bead tip on page 23.

Jump rings: These are small metal rings with a split, allowing them to be opened and closed. They are most often used to connect two different items, like a bead tip and a clasp. See how to work with jump rings on page 23.

Clasp: This is any closure used to attach the ends of a finished project. Clasps come with two halves, one to be attached to each end of a completed jewelry piece.

The Multiple Warp Method

Warp the Loom
Use this warping method for longer woven pieces, 7½" (19cm) long or longer.

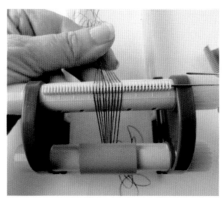

1 Cut the number of warp threads desired to the length of the woven piece plus 16" (40.5cm). Group the threads on one winding beam and secure them in place with a holder. Pull gently on the threads to ensure they are held in place. Trim the ends to about ¼" (0.5cm) from the holder.

2 Position each warp thread into a grove on the warp guide beam. Then, slide the warp thread stopper over the threads through the holes in the grooves.

3 Turn the loom so you can work on the other end. Comb the loose ends of the warp threads with the serrated edge of the holder to separate them. Repeat Step 2 with the loose ends of the warp threads and the other end of the loom, placing the loose threads in the grooves directly opposite the secured ends. Do not secure the threads with a holder yet.

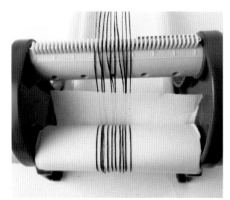

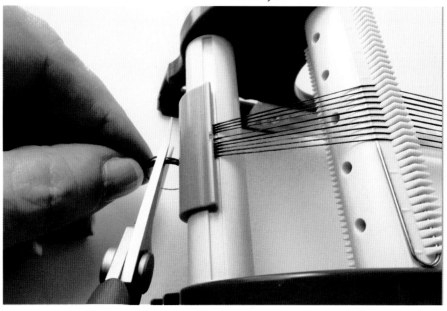

4 Wind the warp threads onto the winding beam with the holder. First, loosen Knob A on the winding beam; then rotate Knob B. To ensure the warp threads wind evenly, place a slip of paper the width of the warp plus ⅜" (1cm) on each side between the warp threads and the winding beam. Wind the threads until a tail approximately 4" (10cm) long is left on the warp threads on the opposite end.

5 Pull the warp threads tight and secure the loose ends onto the second winding beam with a holder. Pull gently on the threads to ensure they are held in place. Trim the ends of the warp threads to about ¼" (0.5cm) from the holder.

6 Wind the warp threads around the second winding beam, adjusting the tension of the warp threads. Then, tighten Knob A on both winding beams to hold the warp threads at the desired tension.

How to Start Weaving

Using the Multiple Warp Method, you must start weaving at the end of the loom that has the least amount of warp thread wrapped around the winding beam (the end without the paper). Once you've identified the proper end at which to begin weaving, you can follow the process described in Weaving with the Standard Loom for the Continuous Warp Method (see page 14).

Hiding Warp & Weft Threads

Weft

To hide the weft threads at the beginning of the woven piece:

1 Pass the needle through 1–3 beads.

2 Pick up the UPPER weft threads for 4–5 rows, beginning at the second row from the end.

3 Pass the needle through the nearest row of beads, and cut the thread at the edge of the last bead.

To hide the weft threads at the end of the woven piece:

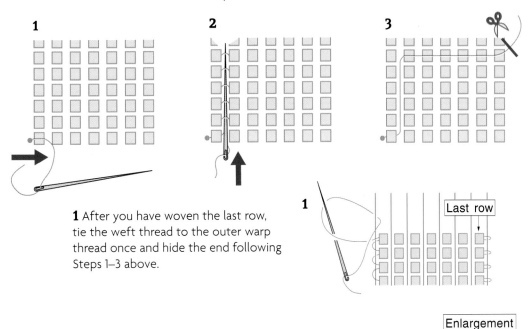

1 After you have woven the last row, tie the weft thread to the outer warp thread once and hide the end following Steps 1–3 above.

Warp

1 Hide the warp threads using the method described in Step 6 of Method A in Hiding Warp & Weft Threads for the Continuous Warp Method (see page 15). If the piece has no increases or decreases, when you pick up the weft threads, start with the second row from the end. Avoid picking up the weft threads in the end row.

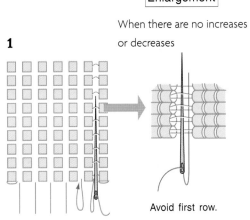

Increasing & Decreasing

This technique allows you to increase or decrease the number of beads in each row, while keeping the weft threads hidden.

Increasing

1 Bring the threaded needle UNDER the warp threads. Pick up the number of beads needed for the increase. For example, if you plan to increase the row by 1 bead at each end, pick up 1 bead. Press the increase bead(s) against the underside of the warp threads, positioning it between the threads, and bring the needle out as shown.

2 Pass the needle through the increase bead(s), eye first. Make sure to pass the needle OVER the warp threads.

3 Insert the needle under the warp threads, pick up the remaining beads needed to complete the row, and position them between the warp threads.

4 Working in the opposite direction, pass the needle, eye first, through all the beads in the row, including the increase bead(s). Repeat these steps as necessary for your project, following the Bead Placement Chart.

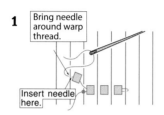

1 Bring needle around warp thread.

Insert needle here.

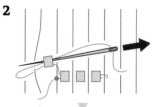

2

Enlargement

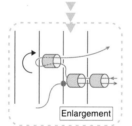

3 Insert needle here. Bring needle out here.

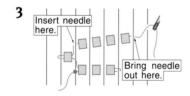

4

Decreasing

1 After completing the row before the decrease, catch the warp thread at the left edge with the needle.

2 Pass the needle through the last bead in the row before the decrease, eye first.

3 Bring the needle underneath the warp threads, and pass it through the beads of the decrease row. Press the beads up between the warp threads.

4 Pass the needle back through the beads of the decrease row, eye first. Repeat these steps as necessary for your project, following the Bead Placement Chart.

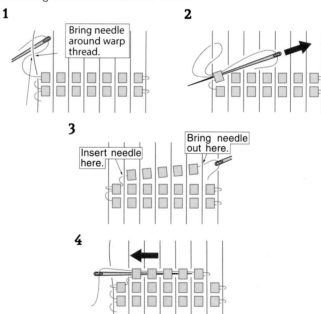

1 Bring needle around warp thread.

2

3 Insert needle here. Bring needle out here.

4

Hiding Warp & Weft Threads

Projects that have a continuous thread for the warp and increases or decreases at both ends can be finished almost the same way as described for Method B on page 16. For these projects, the warp threads cannot be pulled down through the piece as described in Step 1 of Method B. Instead, the loops formed by the warp threads must be trimmed at both ends of the project. Then, the individual warp threads can be hidden in the design following Steps 2–4 of Method B. Hide the weft threads following Figure 4 of Method A.

Additional Techniques

Dividing a Woven Piece

1 When you reach the point at which the work is to be divided, continue weaving the left side of the piece until you reach the end of the working warp section.

2 Add a new weft thread to weave the right side of the piece, hiding the end of the thread in the weaving as shown.

3 Use the new weft thread to weave the right side of the piece. When the right side is the same length as the left side, wind the woven piece around the winding beam to expose another working section of warp threads, and continue weaving both sides separately.

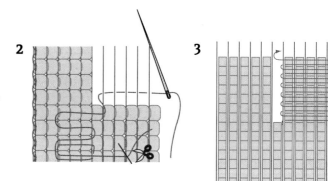

Joining the Ends of a Necklace

1 To begin, hide the inner warp threads as shown by passing the warp threads from one end of the necklace through several rows of the weft threads on the other end of the necklace. Then, pass the warp threads through the closest row of beads and trim. Avoid passing the needle through the same beads twice. Do this with the inner warp threads of each end of the necklace (see Figures 1–3).

2 Hide the outer warp threads by weaving them through several rows of beads on the opposite end of the necklace as shown. Trim the excess (see Figures 4–5).

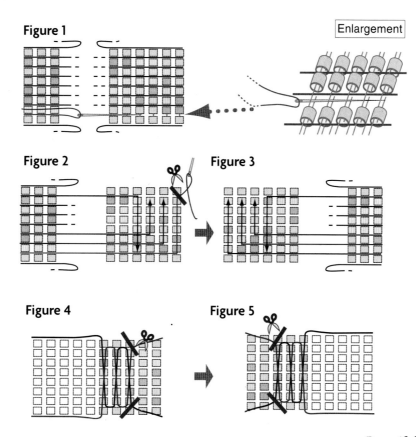

Figure 1   Enlargement

Figure 2   **Figure 3**

Figure 4   **Figure 5**

Attaching Fringe to a Straight Edge

1 Insert the needle in the third bead from the left in the end row, and bring it out at the second to last bead in the row. Leave a 6" (15cm) tail, and secure it with tape.

2 Following the project fringe chart, pick up the beads for the fringe.

3 Starting with the second bead from the bottom, pass the needle back through the fringe beads. You can also try the picot option by passing the needle back through the fringe beads starting with the fourth bead from the bottom.

4 Make the remaining fringe strands by repeating Steps 2 & 3 until you reach the edge of the woven piece.

5 After you've attached the last fringe strand, remove the tape from the beginning thread tail and tie the thread ends together tightly 2–3 times.

6 Run the thread ends through a few rows of beads and trim as shown.

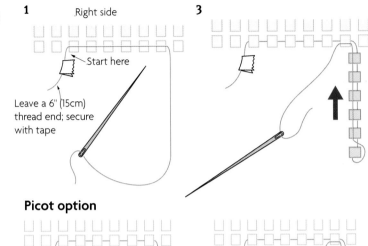

1 Right side · Start here · Leave a 6" (15cm) thread end; secure with tape · **3**

Picot option

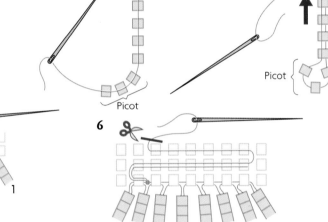

Picot · Picot · **6**

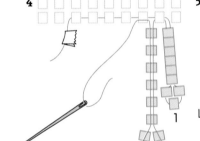

4 · 1 · 2

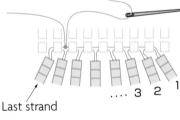

5 · Last strand · 3 2 1

Attaching Fringe to Increases & Decreases

1 Thread the needle through the first row of beads where fringe will be added, bringing it out at the right edge. Leave a 6" (15cm) tail, and secure it with tape.

2 Following the project fringe chart, pick up the beads for the fringe.

3 Starting with the second bead from the bottom, pass the needle back through the fringe beads. You can also try the picot option by passing the needle back through the fringe beads starting with the fourth bead from the bottom. Or, for a variation, the sixth bead from the bottom.

4 Thread the needle back through the beads in the first row, and then through two to three beads in the row below as shown, bringing it out at the right edge where the next fringe strand will be added.

5 Attach the remaining fringe to the right side of the woven piece by repeating Steps 2–4 until you reach the bottom row. After making the last fringe strand on the right side, thread the needle through the bottom row, bringing it out on the left side.

6 Repeat Steps 2–5, working from the bottom row up, to attach fringe strands to the left side. Repeat Steps 5 & 6 of Attaching Fringe to a Straight Edge above to secure the thread ends.

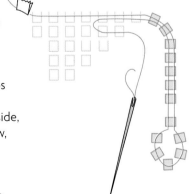

Sewing Side Seams

1 Fold the woven piece where indicated on the Bead Placement Chart. Pass a needle threaded with approximately 12" (30.5cm) of thread through the row of beads at the fold. Leave about half the length of the thread as a tail, securing it with a piece of tape.

2 Stitch one edge of the folded section together, weaving the needle through the beads as shown.

3 Hide the working end of the thread as shown. Remove the tape from the thread tail and repeat Steps 2 & 3 for the other side seam, using the thread tail.

Back

1

Center of thread

Tape here

2

3

Attaching Jewelry Findings

Attaching a bead tip
1 Pass the thread through the bead tip and then through a bead. Knot the thread 2–3 times and apply a drop of glue. Trim the end.

2 Close the bead tip around the bead and thread end.

3 Form a ring using round-nose pliers. Make sure the ring is completely closed.

Working with jump rings
Make sure the ring is tightly closed with no space showing between the ends.

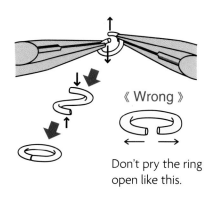

《 Wrong 》

Don't pry the ring open like this.

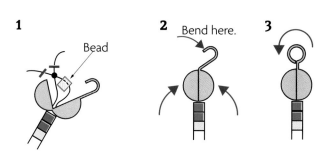

1

Bead

2 Bend here.

3

Flag Pins

By Carol C. Porter

COLOR KEY:

USA, United Kingdom: ■ Red □ White ■ Blue

Germany: ■ Red ■ Black □ Yellow

Japan: ■ Red □ White

Brazil: ■ Green □ Yellow ■ Blue □ White

Italy: ■ Red □ White ■ Green

LOOM: Mini

TECHNIQUES: Continuous Warp

USA, UNITED KINGDOM, GERMANY, JAPAN:

BEADS: 20 across

WARP: 21

BRAZIL, ITALY:

BEADS: 21 across

WARP: 22

SUPPLIES

- 11/0 round beads (USA, United Kingdom, Germany, Japan; see color key)
- 11/0 cylindrical beads (Brazil, Italy; see color key)
- White thread
- Felt
- Pin back
- Glue
- Scissors

1. Warp the mini loom with 1 continuous thread to form the number of warp strands listed for your desired flag using the Continuous Warp Method (see page 9).
2. Weave the design following the Bead Placement Chart for your desired flag (see page 25).
3. Hide warp and weft threads using Method A (see page 15).
4. Cut a piece of felt to the same size as the flag pin. Glue the felt piece to the back of the pin.
5. Glue a pin back to the felt.

Bead Placement Chart USA

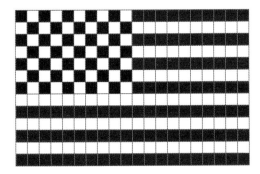

Bead Placement Chart United Kingdom

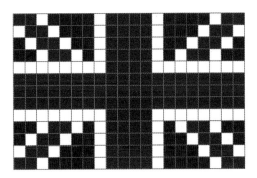

Bead Placement Chart Brazil

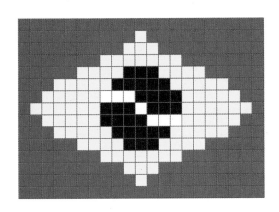

Bead Placement Chart Germany

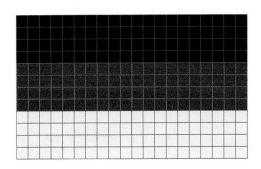

Bead Placement Chart Japan

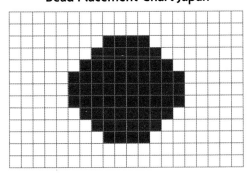

Bead Placement Chart Italy

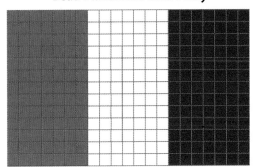

Quilt Block Designs

By Carol C. Porter

LOOM: Mini
TECHNIQUES: Continuous Warp, Picot Fringe
BEADS: 18 across (Shadows), 12 across (Churn Dash), 16 across (Log Cabin), 12 across (Flying Geese), 18 across (Basket)
WARP: 19 (Shadows), 13 (Churn Dash), 17 (Log Cabin), 13 (Flying Geese), 19 (Basket)
SUPPLIES
- 11/0 cylindrical beads (see Color Key)
- For Shadows: beige thread
- For Churn Dash: gray thread
- For Log Cabin: white thread
- For Flying Geese: black thread
- For Basket: white thread
- Felt, pin backs, pre-made necklace chains, bails, or earring posts depending on desired project
- Glue
- Scissors

COLOR KEY: Shadows: ☐ Matte cream
▨ Matte sea opal ▨ Galvanized honey wine
▨ Dark turquoise ▨ Matte copper

For Shadows necklace:

1. Warp the mini loom with 1 continuous thread to form 19 warp strands using the Continuous Warp Method (see page 9).
2. Weave the design following the Bead Placement Chart (see at left).
3. Hide the warp and weft threads using Method A (see page 15).
4. Use the method described in Attaching Fringe to a Straight Edge (see page 22) to add a fringe to the bottom of the woven piece, following the Bead Fringe Chart.
5. Cut a piece of felt to the same size as the woven piece.
6. Make 2 parallel slits in the felt, and feed the necklace chain through the slits. Then glue the felt to the back of the woven piece.

Bead Placement Chart Shadows

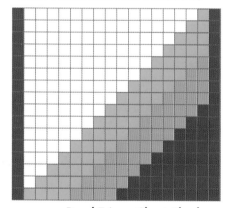

Bead Fringe Chart Shadows

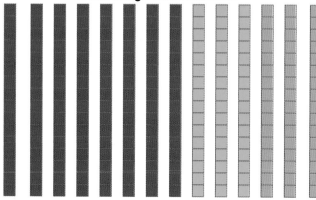

← Start

COLOR KEY: Churn Dash: ☐ Silver ■ Red ■ Black

For Churn Dash necklace:

1. Warp the mini loom with 1 continuous thread to form 13 warp strands using the Continuous Warp Method (see page 9).
2. Weave the design following the Bead Placement Chart (see at left).
3. Hide the warp and weft threads using Method A (see page 15).
4. Attach a bail to the top of the woven piece by making a beaded connector like the ones used for the Ohio Star necklace on page 29. Center the beaded connector on the top edge of the woven piece and thread the bail onto it. Attach a second bail to the first and thread a purchased necklace chain through it (see photo on page 26).

Bead Placement Chart Churn Dash

COLOR KEY: Log Cabin: ☐ White ▨ Red ■ Black ▨ Pink ▨ Peach ▨ Orange ☐ Yellow ▨ Mossy green ▨ Chartreuse ▨ Pea green ▨ Metallic green ▨ Light blue ▨ Light sapphire ▨ Matte sapphire ■ Dark sapphire

Bead Placement Chart Log Cabin

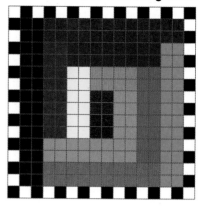

For Log Cabin pin:

1. Warp the mini loom with 1 continuous thread to form 17 warp strands using the Continuous Warp Method (see page 9).
2. Weave the design following the Bead Placement Chart (see at right).
3. Hide the warp and weft threads using Method A (see page 15).
4. Cut a piece of felt to the same size as the woven piece.
5. Stitch or glue a pin back to the felt piece. Then glue the felt to the back of the piece.

Bead Placement Chart Basket

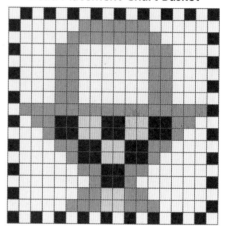

COLOR KEY: Basket: ☐ Cream ▨ Galvanized honey wine ■ Blue ☐ Metallic yellow

For Basket pin:

1. Warp the mini loom with 1 continuous thread to form 19 warp strands using the Continuous Warp Method (see page 9).
2. Weave the design following the Bead Placement Chart (see at right).
3. Hide the warp and weft threads using Method A (see page 15).
4. Follow Steps 4-5 of the Log Cabin pin to finish the piece.

COLOR KEY: Flying Geese ▨ Fuchsia ▨ Green ■ Purple ☐ Gold

Bead Placement Chart Flying Geese

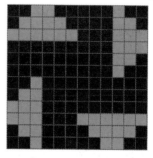

For Flying Geese earrings:

1. Warp the mini loom with 1 continuous thread to form 13 warp strands using the Continuous Warp Method (see page 9).
2. Weave the design following the Bead Placement Chart (see at right).
3. Hide the warp and weft threads using Method A (see page 15).
4. Use the method described in Attaching Fringe to a Straight Edge (see page 22) to add fringe to the bottom of the woven piece, following the Bead Fringe Chart.
5. Repeat Steps 1–4 to create a second earring.
6. Cut 2 pieces of felt to the same size as the earrings. Glue a felt piece to the back of each earring.
7. Glue an earring post to the felt.

Bead Fringe Chart Flying Geese

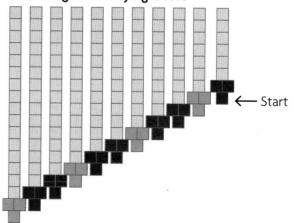

← Start

Ohio Star Pendant Necklace

By Carol C. Porter

COLOR KEY: ☐ Metallic gold ■ Metallic purple ▨ Metallic lavendar

LOOM: Mini or Standard
TECHNIQUES: Continuous Warp, Straight Edge Finish
BEADS: 15 across
WARP: 16
SUPPLIES

- 11/0 round beads (see Color Key)
- Assorted beads for necklace strand
- Beige thread
- Beading needle & threader
- Scissors
- 2 bead tips
- 2 jump rings
- 1 closure set

1. Warp the mini or standard loom with 1 continuous thread to form 16 warp strands using the Continuous Warp Method (see page 9 or 13).
2. Weave the design following the Bead Placement Chart (see at right).
3. Hide the warp and weft threads using Method A (see page 15).
4. To finish, measure the desired length of one side of the necklace strand and add 5" (12.5cm). Cut two threads to this length. Thread the needle with both strands and string on the assorted beads to form one half of the necklace strand, leaving approximately a 3" (7.5cm) tail. Attach the strand to the necklace by threading the tail ends into the beads at the top of the pendant as shown. Tie the ends together and hide the thread. Repeat to form the other side of the necklace strand. Attach bead tips and jump rings to the ends of the strands using the methods described on page 23. Then, add the clasp.

Bead Placement Chart

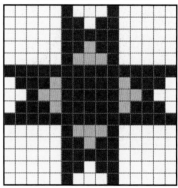

Attaching Necklace to Pendant

"Bead-Tangle" Pendant Necklace

By Fran Ortmeyer

COLOR KEY: ■ Black ▨ Red □ Silver

LOOM: Standard
TECHNIQUES: Continuous Warp, Straight Edge Finish
BEADS: 32 across
WARP: 33
SUPPLIES

- 11/0 cylindrical beads (see Color Key)
- Black thread
- Beading needle & threader
- Pre-purchased black suede cord necklace
- Scissors

Bead Placement Chart

Flap

1. Warp the standard loom with 1 continuous thread to form 33 warp strands using the Continuous Warp Method (see page 13).
2. Weave the design following the Bead Placement Chart (see below).
3. Hide the warp and weft threads using Method A (see page 15).
4. Attach the pendant to the necklace strand by sewing the flap. To do this, turn the woven piece to the wrong side. Using a single thread, pass the needle through the beads in the first row and the last row of the flap section twice to secure a fold in the flap. Tie the thread ends together securely and hide them in the woven piece.

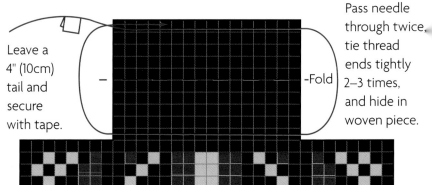

Leave a 4" (10cm) tail and secure with tape.

Fold

Pass needle through twice, tie thread ends tightly 2–3 times, and hide in woven piece.

Sunflower Pendant Necklace

By Carol C. Porter
Finished size: 24" (61cm) long

COLOR KEY: ▨ Light sapphire ▨ Opaque cherry ▨ Green ▨ Orange ▨ Chartreuse ▨ Dark sapphire ▨ Light yellow ▨ Sea opal

LOOM: Mini
TECHNIQUES: Continuous Warp, Straight Edge Finish, Picot Fringe
BEADS: 18 across
WARP: 19
SUPPLIES

- 11/0 cylindrical beads (see Color Key)
- Assorted 6/0 beads for necklace strand
- 2 crimp beads
- 1 closure set
- White thread
- Beading needle & threader
- Scissors

1. Warp the mini loom with 1 continuous thread to form 19 warp strands using the Continuous Warp Method (see page 9).
2. Weave the design following the Bead Placement Chart (see at left).
3. Hide the warp and weft threads using Method A (see page 15).
4. Use the method described in Attaching Fringe to a Straight Edge (see page 22) to add fringe to the bottom of the necklace, following the Bead Fringe Chart.
5. To finish, measure the desired length of one side of the necklace strand and add 5" (12.5cm). Cut two threads to this length. Attach both strands to one side of the necklace by threading about 3" (7.5cm) of the tail end of each strand into the beads at the top of the pendant as shown. Tie the thread ends together and hide them. Thread the needle with both strands and string on the 6/0 beads as desired to form one half of the necklace strand. Repeat to form the other side of the necklace strand. Attach the clasp using the crimp beads.

Bead Placement Chart

Bead Fringe Chart

Start

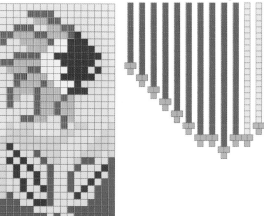

Attaching Necklace to Pendant

Silver & Blue Stripe Bracelet

By Fran Ortmeyer
Finished size: 5" (12.5cm) long

COLOR KEY: ▢ Silver ■ Metallic dark blue

LOOM: Standard
TECHNIQUES: Continuous Warp, Straight Edge Finish, 1 Bead & Multi-Loop Closure
BEADS: 10 across
WARP: 11
SUPPLIES
- 11/0 cylindrical beads (see Color Key)
- Gray thread
- Beading needle & threader
- Scissors
- Flat silver bead for closure

Bead Placement Chart

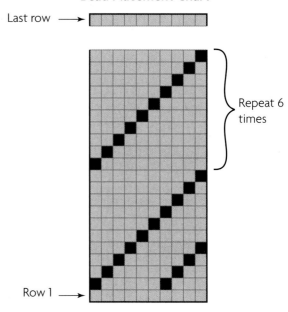

Last row →

Repeat 6 times

Row 1 →

1. Warp the standard loom with 1 continuous thread to form 11 warp strands using the Continuous Warp Method (see page 13).
2. Weave the design following the Bead Placement Chart (at right).
3. Hide the warp and weft threads using Method A (see page 15).
4. Attach the bead and multi-loop closure as shown to the ends of the bracelet. You may shorten or lengthen the bracelet by altering the multi-loop closure as desired.

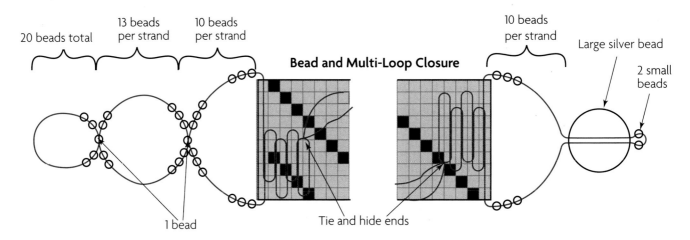

20 beads total

13 beads per strand

10 beads per strand

Bead and Multi-Loop Closure

10 beads per strand

Large silver bead

2 small beads

1 bead

Tie and hide ends

Oriental Fret Ornament Bracelet

By Carol C. Porter

Finished size: 6" (15cm) long, ½" (1.5cm) closure

COLOR KEY:

Design 1: ☐ Cream ▨ Turquosie ■ Black ▨ Tan

Design 2: ■ Opaque navy blue ■ Opaque red
▨ Opaque yellow ▨ Opaque green

LOOM: Standard
TECHNIQUES: Continuous Warp, Straight Edge Finish, 2 Bead & Loop Closures
BEADS: 15 across
WARP: 16
SUPPLIES

- 11/0 round beads (Design 1; see Color Key)
- 11/0 cylindrical beads (Design 2; see Color Key)
- Black thread (Design 1 and 2)
- Beading needle & threader
- Scissors
- 2 black beads for closure (Design 1)
- 2 yellow beads for closure (Design 2)

Bead Placement Chart Design 1

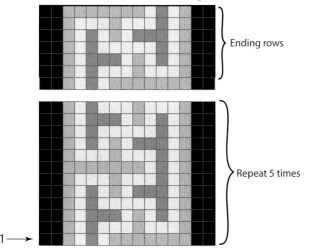

Ending rows

Repeat 5 times

Row 1 →

Bead Placement Chart Design 2

Last row →

Row 1 →

Repeat 7 times

1. Warp the standard loom with 1 continuous thread to form 16 warp strands using the Continuous Warp Method (see page 13)
2. Weave the design following the Bead Placement Chart (see at left).
3. Hide the warp and weft threads using Method A (see page 15).
4. Attach the bead and loop closures. For the loops, weave in the end of a piece of thread, string on 15 beads, and then weave in the other end as shown. For the beads, weave in the end of a piece of thread, and string on 2 small beads, 1 large bead, and 2 small beads. Feed the thread back through the large bead and first 2 small beads. Then, weave in the end.

Attach Bead & Loop Closure

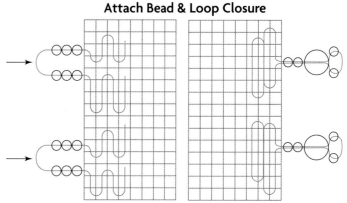

15 beads →

15 beads →

Turquoise & Brown Bracelet & Earring Set

By Carol C. Porter

COLOR KEY: ☐ Gold ▨ Blue ▦ Turquoise ■ Brown

Finished size: 5½" (14cm) long, 1" (2.5cm) closure (bracelet)

LOOM: Mini and Standard
TECHNIQUES: Continuous Warp, Straight Edge Finish, Finding Attachments
BEADS: 13 across (bracelet), 9 across (earrings)
WARP: 14 (bracelet), 10 (earrings)
SUPPLIES
- 11/0 cylindrical beads (see Color Key)
- Dark brown thread
- Beading needle & threader
- 10 bead tips
- 2 three-hole headers
- 2 two-hole headers
- 1 clasp set
- 1 pair earring wires

For bracelet:

1. Warp the standard loom with 1 continuous thread to form 14 warp strands using the Continuous Warp Method (see page 13)
2. Weave the design following the Bead Placement Chart (see at right). Length adjustments can be made at rows 1–5 or between rows 35–41.
3. Hide the weft threads. Divide the warp threads into 3 groups. Feed the groups into the bead tips. Tie the ends of each group into a knot inside the bead tips. Attach the 3-hole headers as shown.
4. Attach the closure to the 3-hole headers.

For earrings:

1. Warp the standard or mini loom with 2 sets of 10 warp strands using the Continuous Warp Method (see page 9 or 13).
2. Weave the design on each set of warp strands following the Bead Placement Chart (see at right) to create 2 earrings.
3. Hide the warp threads on the bottom of the earrings only. Hide all the weft threads.
4. Divide the top warp threads into 2 groups and feed them through the bead tips. Tie off the ends of the threads, and attach 2-hole headers, following the same method as with the bracelet.
5. Attach the earring wires to the 2-hole headers.

Bracelet Bead Placement Chart Bracelet

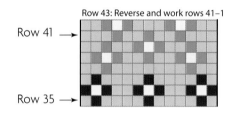

Row 43: Reverse and work rows 41–1

Row 41 →

Row 35 →

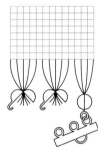

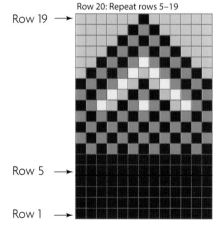

Row 20: Repeat rows 5–19

Row 19 →

Row 5 →

Row 1 →

Bead Placement Chart Earrings: Make 2

'20s-Style Necklace & Earrings

By Fran Ortmeyer

Finished size: 27" (68.5cm) long

COLOR KEY: ☐ Gold ■ Black

LOOM: Mini and Standard
TECHNIQUES: Continuous Warp, Straight Edge Finish
BEADS: 20 across (necklace), 16 across (earrings)
WARP: 21 (necklace), 17 (earrings)
SUPPLIES

- 11/0 round beads (see Color Key)
- Black thread
- Beading needle & threader
- Scissors

For necklace:

- 6 strands of crystal beads
- 2 round black "bling" beads
- 4 rondels, 24k gold
- 2 cones
- 1 gold closure set

For earrings:

- Black felt
- 2 post earring backs

For necklace:

1. Warp the standard loom with 1 continuous thread to form 21 warp strands using the Continuous Warp Method (see page 13).
2. Weave the design following the Bead Placement Chart (see at left).
3. Hide the warp and weft threads using Method A (see page 15). Repeat Steps 1–3 to make 4 necklace pieces total.
4. Assemble the necklace as shown. For the center beaded strands use the following number of beads: 50, 45, and 35. For the beaded strands at each end of the necklace use: 27, 19, and 15 beads. Thread the strands at each end through a bead cone before attaching the clasp.

For earrings:

1. Warp the mini loom with 1 continuous thread to form 17 warp strands using the Continuous Warp Method (see page 9).
2. Weave the design following the Bead Placement Chart (see at left).
3. Hide the warp and weft threads using Method A (see page 15). Repeat Steps 1–3 to create a second earring.
4. Cut 2 pieces of felt to the same size as the earrings. Glue a felt piece to the back of each earring.
5. Glue an earring post to the felt.

Necklace Assembly

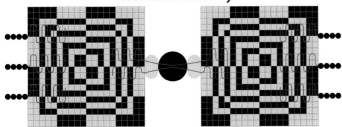

Bead Placement Chart Necklace: Make 4

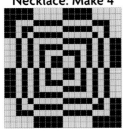

Bead Placement Chart Earrings: Make 2

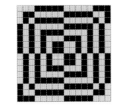

Random Sampler Cuff Bracelet

By Alyssa Vargas

COLOR KEY: ■ Black ▨ Chartreuse ☐ White

1. Warp the standard loom with 1 continuous thread to form 23 warp strands using the Continuous Warp Method (see page 13).
2. Weave the design following the Bead Placement Chart (at right).
3. Hide the warp and weft threads using Method A (see page 15).
4. Trim the leather cuff to size, and, using black sewing thread, sew the woven piece onto the leather.
5. Place three eyelets on each end of cuff. Thread the leather cord through the eyelets to form a lace-up closure.

LOOM: Standard
TECHNIQUES:
Continuous Warp, Straight Edge Finish, Attached Leather Cuff
BEADS: 22 across
WARP: 23
SUPPLIES
- 11/0 round beads (see Color Key)
- Black thread
- Beading needle & threader
- Lightweight black leather remnant, 9" x 3" (23 x 7.5cm)
- Leather needle
- Black sewing thread
- Black leather cord
- 6 eyelets
- Eyelet setting tools

Bead Placement Chart

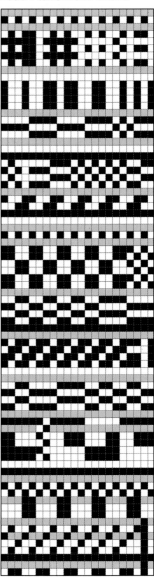

Bookmark

By Fran Ortmeyer

COLOR KEY: ☐ Matte white ▨ Lavender ■ Dark purple

LOOM: Mini
TECHNIQUES:
Continuous Warp, Increasing and Decreasing
BEADS: 9 across
WARP: 10
SUPPLIES
- 11/0 cylindrical beads (see Color Key)
- Black thread
- Beading needle & threader
- Scissors

1. Warp the mini loom with 2 sets of 10 warp strands using the Continuous Warp Method (see page 9).
2. Weave the design on each set of warp strands following the Bead Placement Chart (see at right) to create 2 bookmark ends.
3. Hide the warp and weft threads using the method described on page 20.
4. Measure the length of your book and add 6"–8" (15–20.5cm). Cut 2 threads to this length. Bead and attach the threads as a connecting chain to the two ends of the bookmark, using two threaded needles.
5. Weave the thread ends of the bookmark chain into the woven bookmark ends as shown.

Bead Placement Chart

Warp the second end next to this end ←

Ataching the Chain to the Bookmark Ends

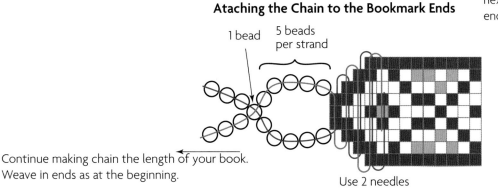

1 bead

5 beads per strand

Continue making chain the length of your book. Weave in ends as at the beginning. ←

Use 2 needles

Ocean Waves Bracelet

By Carol C. Porter

COLOR KEY: ☐ White ☐ Silver ☐ Aqua ☐ Turquoise

Finished size: 5" (12.5cm) long, 1" (2.5cm) closure

LOOM: Standard
TECHNIQUES: Continuous Warp, Increasing and Decreasing
BEADS: 16 across
WARP: 17
SUPPLIES

- 11/0 cylindrical beads (see Color Key)
- Gray thread
- Beading needle & threader
- Scissors
- 2 bead tips
- 2 jump rings
- 1 toggle closure

Bead Placement Chart

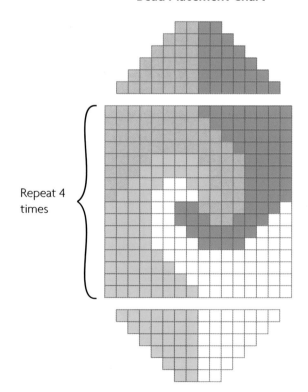

Repeat 4 times

1. Warp the standard loom with 1 continuous thread to form 17 warp strands using the Continuous Warp Method (see page 13).
2. Weave the design following the Bead Placement Chart (see at right).
3. Hide the warp and weft threads using the method described on page 20.
4. Attach the findings using the method described on page 23.

Black-White Color Block Bracelet

By Carol C. Porter

COLOR KEY: ☐ White ▨ Silver ■ Black ☐ Clear

Finished size: 6" (15cm) long, 1" (2.5cm) closure

Bead Placement Chart

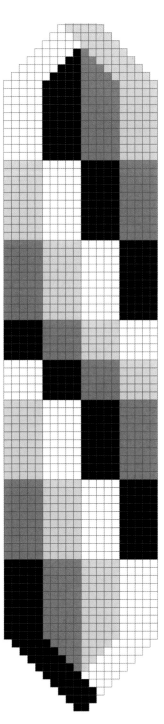

LOOM: Standard
TECHNIQUES:
Continuous Warp,
Increasing and
Decreasing
BEADS: 20 across
WARP: 21

SUPPLIES

- 11/0 cylindrical beads (see Color Key)
- White thread
- Beading needle & threader
- Scissors
- 2 bead tips
- 2 jump rings
- 1 closure set

1. Warp the standard loom with 1 continuous thread to form 21 warp strands using the Continuous Warp Method (see page 13).
2. Weave the design following the Bead Placement Chart (at left).
3. Hide the warp and weft threads using the method described on page 20.
4. Attach the findings using the method described on page 23.

Sunshine in the Forest Bracelet

By Carol C. Porter

Finished size: 8" (20.5cm) long

COLOR KEY: ■ Sage green ■ Brown ■ Metallic gold

LOOM: Mini

TECHNIQUES: Continuous Warp, Increasing and Decreasing

BEADS: 10 across (large segments), 6 across (small segments)

WARP: 11 (large segments), 7 (small segments)

SUPPLIES

- 11/0 cylindrical beads (see Color Key)
- Brown thread
- 1 large and 2 small Kazuri beads
- Beading needle & threader
- Scissors
- 2 crimp beads
- 2 bead caps
- 1 closure set

For large segments:

1. Warp the mini loom with 1 continuous thread to form 11 warp strands using the Continuous Warp Method (see page 9).
2. Tie the weft thread onto warp strand #5 and weave the design following the Bead Placement Chart (see below). Note: You may shorten or lengthen the bracelet by increasing or decreasing the number of rows here.
3. Hide warp and weft threads using the method described on page 20.
4. Repeat Steps 1–3 to create a second large segment.

For small segments:

1. Warp the mini loom with 1 continuous thread to form 7 warp strands using the Continuous Warp Method (see page 9).
2. Tie the weft thread onto warp strand #3 and weave the design following the Bead Placement Chart (see below).
3. Hide warp and weft threads using the method described on page 20.
4. Repeat Steps 1–3 to create a second small segment.

Assembly

1. Assemble the bracelet segments and Kazuri beads as shown below.
2. Attach the findings using the method described on page 23.

Bead Placement Chart Large Segment: Make 2

← Start on warp strand #5

Bead Placement Chart Small Segment: Make 2

← Start on warp strand #3

Fit for a Princess Jewelry Set

By Carol C. Porter

COLOR KEY: ▦ Light pink ▢ Orange ▨ Fuchsia ▨ Blue

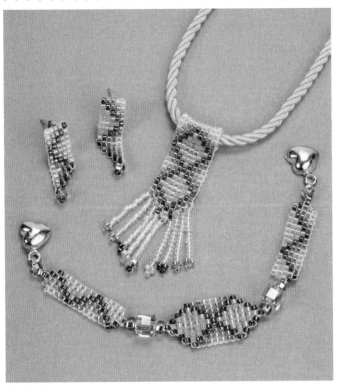

LOOM: Mini

TECHNIQUES: Continuous Warp, Increasing and Decreasing, Picot Fringe

BEADS: 5 across (earrings), 9 across (necklace), 9 across (bracelet center), 5 across (bracelet sides)

WARP: 6 (earrings), 10 (necklace), 10 (bracelet center), 6 (bracelet sides)

SUPPLIES

- 11/0 cylindrical beads (see Color Key)
- White thread
- Beading needle & threader
- Scissors

For earrings:

- Felt
- 2 large beads (6/0)
- 2 small earring posts

For necklace:

- Purchased cord necklace

For bracelet:

- 2 pink beads (8/0)
- 6 large beads (6/0)
- 4 crimp beads
- 1 magnetic closure set

For earrings:

1. Warp the mini loom with 1 continuous thread to form 6 warp strands using the Continuous Warp Method (see page 9).
2. Weave the design following the Bead Placement Chart (see at right).
3. Hide the warp and weft threads using Method B (see page 16). Repeat Steps 1–3 to create a second earring.
4. Add a 6/0 bead to the tip of each earring as shown below.
5. Cut 2 pieces of felt to the same size as the earrings. Glue a felt piece to the back of each earring.
6. Glue an earring post to the felt.

Bead Placement Chart and Assembly Earrings: Make 2

Bracelet Assembly

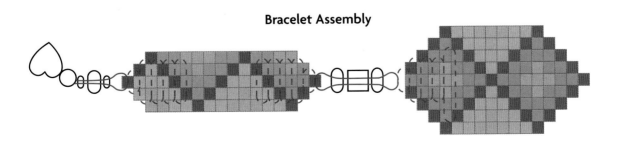

For necklace:

1. Warp the mini loom with 1 continuous thread to form 10 warp strands using the Continuous Warp Method (see page 9).
2. Tie the weft thread onto warp strand #5 and weave the design following the Bead Placement Chart (see below).
3. Hide the warp and weft threads using Method B (see page 16).
4. Use the method described in Attaching Fringe to a Straight Edge (see page XX) to add picot fringe to the bottom of the necklace, following the Bead Fringe Chart.
5. Attach the pendant to the necklace cord following the same method used for Step 4 of the "Bead-Tangle" Pendant Necklace (page 30). Pass a thread twice through the beads in the first row and the last row of the flap section to secure a fold in the flap. Tie the thread ends together securely and hide them in the woven piece (see page 30).

For bracelet:

Center

1. Warp the mini loom with 1 continuous thread to form 10 warp strands using the Continuous Warp Method (see page 9).
2. Tie the weft thread onto warp strand #5 and weave the design following the Bead Placement Chart (see below).
3. Hide the warp and weft threads using the method described on page 20.

Sides

1. Warp the mini loom with 1 continuous thread to form 6 warp strands using the Continuous Warp Method (see page 9).
2. Tie the weft thread onto warp strand #3 and weave the design following the Bead Placement Chart (see below). Note: You may shorten or lengthen the bracelet by increasing or decreasing the number of rows here.
3. Hide the warp and weft threads using the method described on page 20. Repeat Steps 1–3 to create a second bracelet side.

Bead Placement Chart Necklace

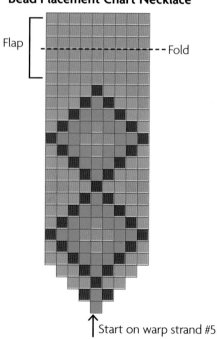

Flap ⟶ - - - - - - - - - - - ⟵ Fold

↑ Start on warp strand #5

Bead Fringe Chart Necklace

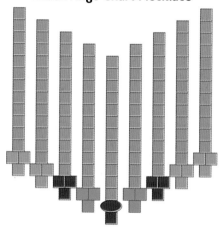

Bead Placement Chart Bracelet Sides: Make 2

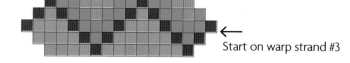

← Start on warp strand #3

Bead Placement Chart Bracelet Center

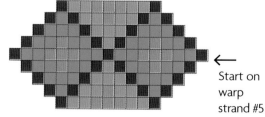

← Start on warp strand #5

Azteca Dance Necklace & Cuff Bracelet

By Carol C. Porter

COLOR KEY: ■ Red □ Light squash ▨ Matte opaque turquoise □ Gold ■ Black   Finished size: 26" (66cm) long

LOOM: Mini and Standard

TECHNIQUES: Continuous Warp, Increasing and Decreasing

BEADS: 15 across (necklace sides), 6 across (necklace connectors), 25 across (bracelet)

WARP: 16 (necklace sides), 7 (necklace connectors), 26 (bracelet)

SUPPLIES

- 11/0 cylindrical beads (see Color Key)
- Beige thread
- Scissors
- Glue

For necklace:

- 5 large beads (Kazuri beads shown)
- 2 ribbon crimps
- 1 closure set

For bracelet:

- Purchased adjustable suede cuff
- Backing (Peltex or crinoline)

Bead Placement Chart Bracelet

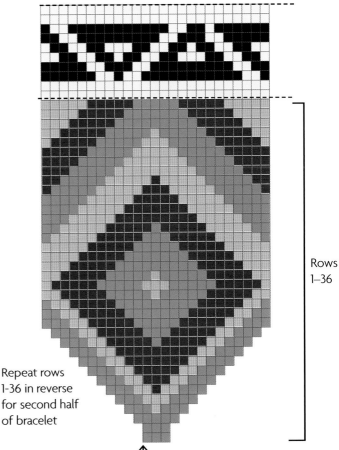

Rows 1–36

Repeat rows 1-36 in reverse for second half of bracelet

↑ Start on warp strand #5

Necklace Assembly

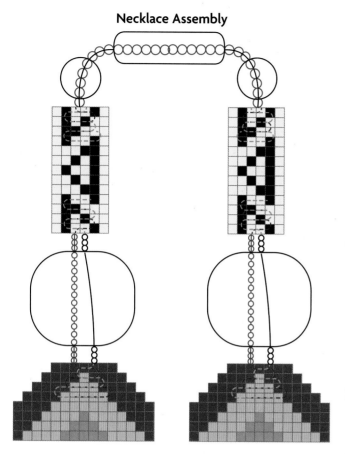

Bead Placement Chart Necklace Sides: Make 2

End

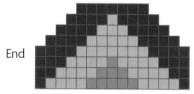

Repeat 7 times

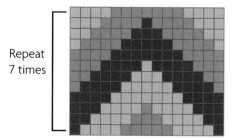

Weave weft thread through warp strands several times

**Bead Placement Chart
Necklace Connectors: Make 2**

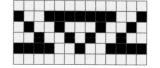

For necklace:

Sides

1. Warp the standard loom with 1 continuous thread to form 16 warp strands using the Continuous Warp Method (see page 13).
2. To provide an area to attach the ribbon crimps, weave the weft thread through the warp threads for several rows. When attaching the ribbon crimps, crimp them onto these thread rows instead of directly onto the beads. Crimping onto the beads may cause breakage.
3. Weave the design following the Bead Placement Chart (see at left).
4. Hide warp and weft threads using Method B (see page 16). Repeat Steps 1–4 to create a second necklace side.

Connectors

1. Warp the mini loom with 1 continuous thread to form 7 warp strands using the Continuous Warp Method (see page 9).
2. Weave the design following the Bead Placement Chart (see at left).
3. Hide the warp and weft threads using Method A (see page 15). Repeat Steps 1–3 to create a second necklace connector.

For bracelet:

1. Warp the standard loom with 1 continuous thread to form 26 warp strands using the Continuous Warp Method (see page 13).
2. Weave the design following the Bead Placement Chart (see page 43).
3. Hide the warp and weft threads using the method described on page 20.
4. Cut a piece of Peltex or crinoline the same size and shape as the woven bracelet and glue it to the back of the bracelet.
5. Glue the covered back of the bracelet to the suede cuff. Allow everything to dry around a tube with a similar circumference to your wrist.

Diamond Drops Necklace & Earrings

By Carol C. Porter

COLOR KEY: ■ Metallic dark bronze bugle ■ Metallic iris bugle ■ Matte Cocoa brown
■ Turquoise ■ 24k gold ■ Dark beige □ Galvanized honey wine

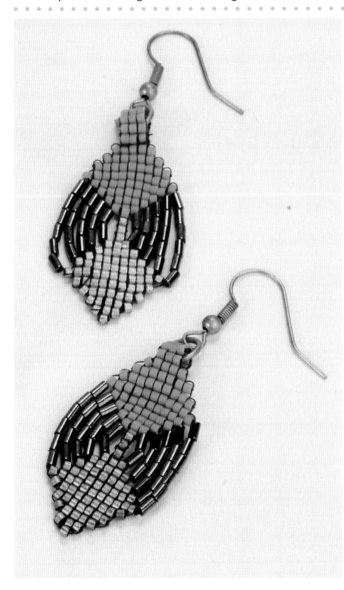

LOOM: Standard
TECHNIQUES: Continuous Warp, Pre-Stringing Beads
BEADS: 19 across (necklace), 11 across (earrings)
WARP: 20 (necklace), 12 (earrings)
SUPPLIES

- 11/0 cylindrical and bugle beads (see Color Key)
- Brown thread
- Ribbon
- Cord
- 1 pair earring backs
- Beading needle & threader

For earrings:

1. Warp the standard loom with 1 continuous thread to form 12 warp strands using the Continuous Warp Method (see page 13). Follow the method described in Step 1 for the necklace to add bugle beads to the warp strands following the Bead Placement Chart. You will need to start adding bugle beads on the very first warp strand.
2. Tie the weft thread onto warp strand #6 and follow Step 2 for the necklace.
3. Hide the warp and weft threads using the method described on page 20.
4. Repeat Steps 1–3 to create a second earring. Attach the earrings to the earring backs following Step 4 for the necklace.

Bead Placement Chart Earrings: Make 2

Flap ┆ ┄┄┄┄┄ ┆ Fold

↑ Start on warp strand #6

Beautiful Bead Weaving   **45**

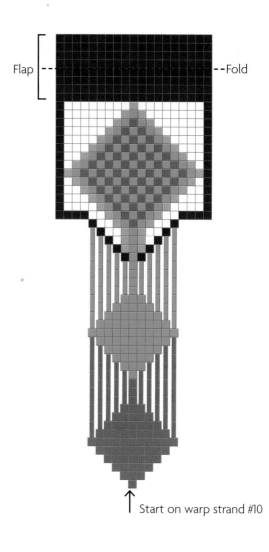

Flap - - - - - - - - - - - - Fold

↑ Start on warp strand #10

For necklace:

1. This design uses the Continuous Warp Method; however, for this project, you will string bugle beads onto the warp thread while you are warping the loom. Warp the standard loom with 1 continuous thread to form 5 warp

strands using the Continuous Warp Method (see page 13). Thread a needle onto the warp thread and begin threading bugle beads onto the thread, following the Bead Placement Chart (see above). Continue to warp the loom, adding bugle beads as directed by the chart. Pay close attention to the chart to ensure you are stringing the correct colors in the proper order and are stringing onto the correct warp strand. These beads will "rest" towards the top of the loom and will be pulled down into the design as directed.

2. Tie the weft thread onto warp strand #10 and weave the design following the Bead Placement Chart (see above), sliding the bugle beads down into the design when needed as indicated by the chart.

3. Hide the warp and weft threads using the method described on page 20.

4. Attach the pendant to the ribbon and cord following the same method used for Step 4 of the "Bead-Tangle" Pendant Necklace (page 30). Pass a thread twice through the beads in the first row and the last row of the flap section to secure a fold in the flap. Tie the thread ends together securely and hide them in the woven piece (see page 30).

Purple & Green Argyle Divided Necklace

By Carol C. Porter

COLOR KEY: ☐ Green ■ Dark green ■ Light purple ■ Dark purple ☐ Gold

LOOM: Standard
TECHNIQUES: Multiple Warp, Divided Necklace, Fringe
BEADS: 24 across
WARP: 25
SUPPLIES

- 11/0 round beads (see Color Key)
- Black thread
- Beading needle & threader
- Scissors

1. Warp the standard loom with 25 threads using the Multiple Warp Method (see page 18).
2. Weave the design following the Bead Placement Chart (see below) and Dividing a Woven Piece (see page 21).
3. Join the ends of the necklace using the warp threads following the method described in Joining the Ends of the Necklace (see page 21).
4. Hide the weft threads using the method described on page 19.
5. Use the method described in Attaching Fringe to a Straight Edge (see page 22) to add a fringe to the bottom of the necklace, following the Bead Fringe Chart.

Bead Fringe Chart

Repeat in reverse for left side of fringe

↑
Start

Repeat until desired length is reached

Bead Placement Chart

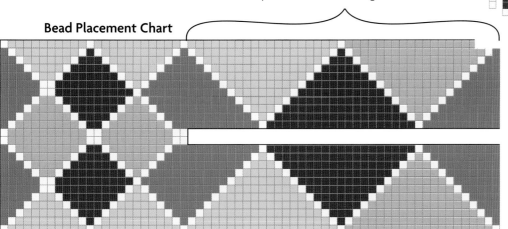

Blue & White Amulet Necklace

By Fran Ortmeyer

COLOR KEY: ☐ Opaque white ■ Dark blue ▩ Light blue

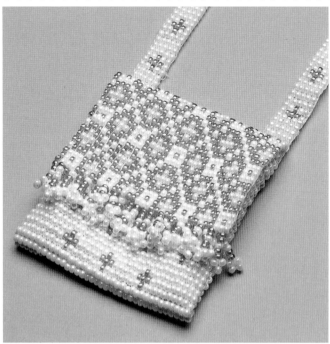

For bag:

1. Warp the standard loom with 37 threads using the Multiple Warp Method (see page 18).
2. Weave the design following the Bead Placement Chart (see at right).
3. Hide the warp and weft threads using the method described on page 19.
4. Use the method described in Attaching Fringe to a Straight Edge (see page 22) to make a picot fringe following the Bead Fringe Chart.
5. Use the method described in Sewing Side Seams (see page 23) to sew the sides of the bag closed.

For strap:

1. Warp the standard loom with six 44" (112cm)-long threads using the Multiple Warp Method (see page 18).
2. Weave the design following the Bead Placement Chart (see at right).
3. Hide the warp and weft threads using the method described on page 19.
4. Attach the strap to the bag using a method similar to sewing the flap for the "Bead-Tangle" Pendant Necklace (page 30). Pass a thread twice through the last row of beads on the strap and the first row of beads on the bag body. Repeat with the remaining end of the strap.

LOOM: Standard
TECHNIQUES: Multiple Warp, Sewing Side Seams, Picot Fringe
BEADS: 36 across (bag), 5 across (strap)
WARP: 37 (bag), 6 (strap)
SUPPLIES
- 11/0 round beads (see Color Key)
- White thread
- Beading needle & threader
- Scissors

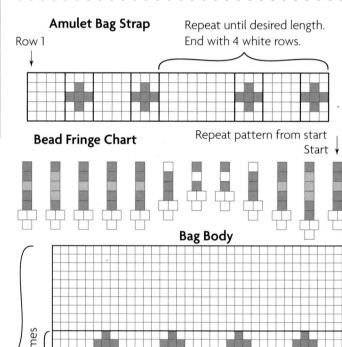

Amulet Bag Strap
Row 1
Repeat until desired length. End with 4 white rows.

Bead Fringe Chart
Repeat pattern from start
Start

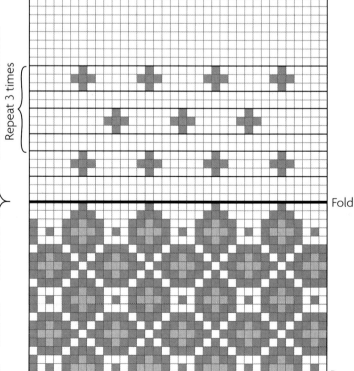

Bag Body

Bag body — Repeat 3 times

Fold

Flap

Row